THE ULTIMATE GUIDE TO

BEING A

FIRST-TIME

HOMEBUYER

Henry Nwaneshiudu

Copyright © 2024 Henry Nwaneshiudu

All rights reserved. No part of this publication may be reproduced, distributed, or transmitted in any form or by any means, including photo-copying, recording, or other electronic or me-chanical methods, without the prior written permission of the publisher, except in the case of brief quotations embodied in critical reviews and certain other noncommercial uses permitted by copyright law.

Table of Contents

Chapter 1: Introduction 1

Chapter 2: Assessing Your Financial Readiness 2

    Budgeting for Your First Home 2

    Credit Score and Its Impact on Mortgages 4

    Understanding Mortgage Options 8

    Choosing the Right Mortgage 13

Chapter 3: Preparing for the Homebuying Process 14

    Deciding Where You Want to Live 14

    Creating a Wishlist: Needs vs. Wants 14

Chapter 4: Mortgage Pre-Approval: Your First Step 18

    The Difference Between Pre-Qualification and Pre-Approval 18

    Documents Needed for Pre-Approval 18

    How Pre-Approval Affects Your Home Search 18

Chapter 5: Choosing the Right Real Estate Agent 19

    Why You Need a Real Estate Agent 19

    How to Find a Good Agent 19

    What to Expect from Your Agent 19

Chapter 6: The House Hunt Begins 20

House Hunting Tips 20

What to Look for in a House 21

Bidding Strategies 23

Chapter 7: Making An Offer On A Home 25

Understanding the Home Offer Process 25

Common Mistakes to Avoid in the Home Offer Process 26

The Role of Contingencies 28

Chapter 8: The Home Inspection 30

Why the Home Inspection Is Crucial 30

How to Hire a Good Home Inspector 31

Negotiating Repairs and Closing Costs After the Inspection . 33

Closing Costs and Negotiations 34

Chapter 9: Securing Your Mortgage 36

Securing Your Mortgage 36

Locking in Your Interest Rate 37

Finalizing Your Mortgage Terms 38

What to Expect During Underwriting 39

Possible Outcomes of Underwriting 41

Chapter 10: Closing The Deal 42

Understanding Closing Costs 42

Reviewing Your Closing Disclosures 44

Preparing for the Final Walkthrough 45

What to Expect on Closing Day 45

Chapter 11: After You Buy 49

Moving In: Step-by-Step 49

Setting Up Utilities and Services 50

Home Maintenance Tips for New Homeowners 51

Personalizing Your New Home 54

Conclusion 56

Chapter 1: Introduction

Buying your first home is a huge milestone. For many, it's the realization of a long-held dream and the key to financial stability. However, it can also feel overwhelming, especially with all the new terms, processes, and financial commitments involved.

This guide is designed to make your journey as a first-time homebuyer as smooth and informed as possible. By the end of this ebook, you'll know what to expect, how to avoid common mistakes, and how to approach each step with confidence.

Chapter 2: Assessing Your Financial Readiness

Before diving into the homebuying process, it's essential to ensure you're financially prepared. Buying a home is not just about affording the purchase price but also being ready for ongoing expenses like maintenance, insurance, and property taxes.

Budgeting for Your First Home

Budgeting for your first home is a crucial step in ensuring that your home buying process is smooth and financially manageable. Here's a guide to help you create a realistic budget:

1. Determine Your Affordability Range

Assess Your Income: Start by looking at your total monthly income. Most financial experts suggest that your mortgage payment should not exceed 25-30% of your gross monthly income.

Evaluate Your Debt: Calculate your debt-to-income (DTI) ratio, which compares your monthly debt payments to your income. Lenders generally prefer a DTI of 36% or less.

Down Payment Considerations: Aim for at least 20% down to avoid private mortgage insurance (PMI), but explore options for lower down payments (FHA loans, for instance, may require as little as 3.5%).

2. Factor in Upfront Costs

Down Payment: This is the largest upfront expense. Typically, this ranges from 3% to 20% of the home's purchase price.

Closing Costs: These can range from 2% to 5% of the home's purchase price and include fees for appraisal, title insurance, attorney fees, and lender charges.

Home Inspection: Don't skip this. It can cost $300-$500 but may save you from future repairs.

Moving Expenses: Budget for moving trucks, packing materials, or hiring a moving company.

3. Ongoing Costs of Homeownership

Mortgage Payments: Principal and interest payments based on your loan terms. Use a mortgage calculator to estimate.

Property Taxes: Varies depending on your location. Research local tax rates to factor this into your monthly payments.

Homeowners Insurance: Typically required by lenders and averages around $1,200 annually, though it depends on factors like location, home value, and coverage needs.

Private Mortgage Insurance (PMI): If your down payment is less than 20%, you may need PMI, which can add $30-$70 per month per $100,000 borrowed.

HOA Fees: If your home is in a community with a homeowners' association, budget for those fees, which can range from $100 to $1,000 or more per year.

Utilities: Include water, electricity, gas, and internet, which can significantly increase your monthly expenses.

4. Maintenance and Repair Fund

Regular Maintenance: Set aside 1-2% of the home's value annually for ongoing maintenance like landscaping, HVAC servicing, and general upkeep.

Emergency Repairs: Have an emergency fund for unexpected repairs such as a broken furnace, roof leaks, or plumbing issues.

5. Plan for Growth

Home Improvements: You may want to budget for upgrades or renovations to customize your home over time.

Future Financial Goals: Balance your homeownership costs with other financial goals like retirement savings, education funds, or investment opportunities.

By thoughtfully budgeting for all aspects of your first home, you'll be better equipped to manage the expenses and enjoy your new investment with less financial stress.

Credit Score and Its Impact on Mortgages

Your credit score plays a significant role in determining whether you'll qualify for a mortgage and what interest rate you'll get. Most lenders require a minimum score of 620, but a higher score will earn you better terms.

Down Payment: How Much Do You Really Need?

When buying a home, your down payment plays a critical role in determining the size of your mortgage, your monthly payments, and the types of loans you qualify for. Here's a detailed look at how much you really need for a down payment:

1. Traditional Down Payment: 20 Rule

Why 20%? Historically, lenders have recommended a 20% down payment. This amount can help you avoid paying Private Mortgage Insurance (PMI), reduce your monthly payments, and give you better loan terms.

Pros:

Avoid PMI, which can save you hundreds of dollars a month.

Smaller mortgage loan, resulting in lower monthly payments.

Potentially better interest rates since the loan is less risky for lenders.

Cons:

It can take years to save up 20%, especially in high-cost real estate markets.

Some buyers might be priced out of the market if they wait too long to save.

2. Lower Down Payment Options

FHA Loans:

Down Payment: As low as 3.5%.

Requirements: Credit score of at least 580 (with 3.5% down); if your credit score is between 500-579, you might still qualify, but you'll need a 10% down payment.

Considerations: FHA loans require an upfront mortgage insurance premium (MIP) and annual MIP payments, which add to the overall cost.

Conventional Loans:

Down Payment: As low as 3%.

Requirements: Generally, a credit score of 620 or higher is needed, but many lenders prefer scores of 680 or above for these low-down-payment loans.

Considerations: PMI is required if your down payment is less than 20%, but it can be removed once you reach 20% equity.

VA Loans:

Down Payment: 0%.

Eligibility: Available to veterans, active-duty military, and some surviving spouses.

Considerations: No down payment or PMI required, but there may be a funding fee (which can be financed into the loan).

USDA Loans:

Down Payment: 0%.

Eligibility: Available to buyers in designated rural areas with moderate to low income.

Considerations: No down payment, but mortgage insurance is required, similar to FHA loans.

3. How Much Should You Put Down?

Less than 20%:

Advantages: Allows you to buy sooner without waiting years to save up. Lower down payments help keep cash in hand for other needs (emergencies, renovations, etc.).

Disadvantages: You'll likely have to pay PMI, which adds to your monthly costs. Additionally, you'll start with less equity in your home, which can leave you more vulnerable if property values decline.

More than 20%:

Advantages: You'll avoid PMI and reduce the size of your loan, which means smaller monthly payments and less interest over the life of the loan.

Disadvantages: Tying up more money in a down payment reduces your liquidity for other investments or financial goals. You might also be left with less cash for emergencies or home improvements.

4. Other Factors to Consider

Loan Type: Different loan programs require different down payments. Conventional loans often require less than 20% down, while FHA, VA, and USDA loans have specific criteria that might let you put down as little as 0-3.5%.

Your Financial Situation: Consider your savings, credit score, income stability, and other debts. If you're financially strong and have an emergency fund in place, a larger down payment might be a good option.

Home Price and Location: The down payment amount will vary depending on the cost of the home and the market you're buying in. In higher-cost areas, even a lower percentage down payment might still be a large amount of money.

Future Goals: Think about your long-term financial goals. If putting more money down means you're stretching your budget too thin, it might be better to put down less and keep more cash on hand for other investments or savings.

5. Creative Down Payment Solutions

Down Payment Assistance Programs: Many states and local governments offer grants, loans, or tax incentives to help with down payments, especially for first-time homebuyers.

Gifted Funds: Some buyers receive down payment assistance from family or friends, which can reduce their required savings. Make sure to check with your lender about the rules for gifted down payments, as some loans have specific requirements.

Saving Strategies: Automated savings plans, setting up a specific down payment savings account, and cutting discretionary spending are common ways to accelerate savings.

Ultimately, the right down payment amount depends on your personal financial situation, the type of loan you're using, and your long-term goals. While 20% is often recommended, many buyers successfully purchase homes with less, taking advantage of available loan options, assistance programs, and financial planning strategies to achieve homeownership.

Understanding Mortgage Options

When buying your first home, understanding your mortgage options is critical to making informed decisions that best suit your financial situation. Here's a guide to help you navigate different types of mortgage loans:

1. Fixed-Rate Mortgage

Definition: This mortgage has an interest rate that remains the same for the entire term of the loan, providing predictable monthly payments.

Loan Terms: Typically available in 15, 20, or 30-year terms.

Pros: Stability in payments, easier budgeting, protection from rising interest rates.

Cons: May have higher interest rates than adjustable-rate mortgages (ARMs) initially, and you're locked into the rate even if market rates drop (unless you refinance).

2. Adjustable-Rate Mortgage (ARM)

Definition: The interest rate on an ARM fluctuates after an initial fixed-rate period, usually every year. Common ARMs include 3/1, 5/1, and 7/1, where the first number represents the years with a fixed rate, and the second number refers to how often the rate can adjust afterward.

Pros: Often starts with lower interest rates than fixed-rate mortgages, which can make initial payments more affordable.

Cons: Rates can increase significantly after the fixed-rate period, leading to higher payments in the future.

3. FHA Loan

Definition: Backed by the Federal Housing Administration (FHA), these loans are designed for lower-income or first-time homebuyers.

Down Payment: As low as 3.5% if your credit score is 580 or higher.

Pros: Low down payment requirements, flexible credit requirements, can be easier to qualify for.

Cons: Requires mortgage insurance premiums (MIP), both upfront and annually, which increases your overall loan cost.

4. VA Loan

Definition: Available to veterans, active military personnel, and some spouses, VA loans are guaranteed by the Department of Veterans Affairs.

Down Payment: Typically no down payment is required.

Pros: No down payment or mortgage insurance requirements, competitive interest rates, flexible qualification guidelines.

Cons: Only available to eligible service members and veterans, and the property must meet specific requirements.

5. USDA Loan

Definition: The U.S. Department of Agriculture offers loans for rural homebuyers with low to moderate incomes.

Down Payment: No down payment is required.

Pros: 100% financing, competitive interest rates, flexible credit guidelines.

Cons: Only available for homes in designated rural areas, and income limits apply.

6. Jumbo Loan

Definition: Jumbo loans are for homebuyers purchasing properties that exceed the conforming loan limits set by Fannie Mae and Freddie Mac, which vary by location but are generally above $726,200 (as of 2024).

Pros: Allows you to purchase high-value properties, can provide competitive interest rates for qualified buyers.

Cons: Stricter credit and income requirements, often higher down payment (usually at least 10-20%), and may have higher interest rates and fees.

7. Interest-Only Mortgage

Definition: With this loan, you only pay the interest on the mortgage for a set period, usually 5 to 10 years, after which you begin paying both principal and interest.

Pros: Lower initial payments, good for buyers who expect higher income in the future or plan to sell the home before the principal payments begin.

Cons: Payments increase significantly once the interest-only period ends, and you don't build equity during the interest-only phase.

8. Conventional Loan

Definition: These are not insured by the government and usually come with stricter credit and income requirements than FHA or VA loans. Conventional loans can be conforming or non-conforming.

Down Payment: Typically ranges from 3% to 20%.

Pros: Lower costs than government-backed loans if you have a strong financial profile, no upfront insurance premiums, flexible term lengths.

Cons: Stricter qualification requirements, requires PMI if the down payment is less than 20%.

9. Balloon Mortgage

Definition: This mortgage involves making small monthly payments for a set period (usually 5 to 7 years), followed by a large "balloon" payment at the end of the term.

Pros: Lower monthly payments initially, can be beneficial if you plan to sell or refinance before the balloon payment is due.

Cons: The large final payment can be risky if you're unable to pay or refinance, and there's less time to build equity.

10. State and Local Programs

Definition: Many states and local governments offer special loan programs for first-time homebuyers, often with down payment assistance, tax credits, or favorable interest rates.

Pros: Can significantly lower upfront costs and ongoing payments, may offer grants or forgivable loans.

Cons: May have income or property location restrictions, and some programs are only available for a limited time.

Choosing the Right Mortgage

To determine the best mortgage for your situation:

Evaluate Your Financial Health: Consider your credit score, down payment capacity, and income stability.

Think Long-Term: Reflect on how long you plan to stay in the home and your future income potential.

Shop Around: Different lenders may offer different rates and terms for the same loan type. Get multiple quotes and compare not just interest rates but also fees and closing costs.

Consult a Professional: A mortgage broker or financial advisor can help you navigate complex mortgage options and find the best fit for your needs.

Understanding these mortgage options can help you choose the best loan for your financial situation and long-term homeownership goals.

Chapter 3: Preparing for the Homebuying Process

Once you've determined that you're financially ready, it's time to think about what you're looking for in a home.

Deciding Where You Want to Live

Start by choosing a location that fits your lifestyle. Consider proximity to work, schools, public transportation, and amenities. Research different neighborhoods, and factor in crime rates, school ratings, and local property values.

Creating a Wishlist: Needs vs. Wants

When buying a home, deciding where you want to live is one of the most crucial steps in the process. Here are some factors to consider when making that decision:

1. Lifestyle Preferences

Urban, Suburban, or Rural: Consider the type of environment you prefer. Urban areas offer proximity to amenities but tend to be busier and more expensive. Suburban areas are quieter, with more space, but may require commuting. Rural areas provide tranquility and lower costs, but can be far from conveniences.

Community Vibe: Look for a neighborhood that aligns with your values. Are you looking for a family-friendly community, a trendy spot with nightlife, or a peaceful area for retirement?

2. Work and Commute

Proximity to Work: Consider how close you want to be to your place of employment. A long commute can take a toll on your lifestyle and finances, so weigh the trade-offs between living further out for more space and being closer to work for convenience.

Transportation: Access to public transportation, highways, or major roads is critical, especially if commuting is a factor.

3. Affordability

Cost of Living: Some areas have a much higher cost of living than others. Research property taxes, utility costs, and general expenses in different neighborhoods.

Home Prices: Compare real estate prices in various areas. Determine your budget and consider where your money will go further while meeting your needs.

4. School Districts

For Families: If you have children or plan to, the quality of the local schools will be a significant factor. Research school ratings and speak with local parents to get their insights.

5. Safety

Crime Rates: Review crime statistics in the neighborhoods you're considering. Feeling safe in your home and community is vital for peace of mind.

Natural Disasters: Consider the area's vulnerability to natural disasters such as floods, hurricanes, or wildfires, and the impact this could have on insurance and lifestyle.

6. Proximity to Amenities

Healthcare, Shopping, and Entertainment: Consider how close you want to be to hospitals, grocery stores, restaurants, parks, and recreational activities. Living near the amenities that are most important to you can improve your quality of life.

Walkability: If you enjoy walking to nearby cafes or shops, check the walkability score of the neighborhoods you're interested in.

7. Future Development

Growth Potential: Investigate the area's growth trends. A growing community may mean increased property values but also increased traffic and noise. Conversely, a stagnant area may offer lower prices but fewer opportunities for resale value appreciation.

8. Cultural and Social Environment

Diversity and Inclusivity: Consider whether the area aligns with your cultural, political, or social preferences. Being in a place where you feel comfortable and accepted can make a big difference in your happiness.

Recreational Opportunities: Think about your hobbies and interests—whether you enjoy outdoor activities, cultural events, or social gatherings—and find a place that supports your lifestyle.

9. Personal and Long-Term Goals

Investment Potential: Are you looking for a home to live in long-term, or do you see this as a stepping stone to another property? Some locations offer better appreciation potential, while others are better for settling down permanently.

Family and Friends: Consider the proximity to your family and social circle. Living near your support system can be a huge benefit, especially during life transitions.

Taking the time to evaluate these factors will help ensure that you not only find a home that fits your needs but also choose a location where you'll thrive for years to come.

Chapter 4: Mortgage Pre-Approval: Your First Step

Before you start house hunting, getting pre-approved for a mortgage should be your first step.

The Difference Between Pre-Qualification and Pre-Approval

Pre-qualification is an estimate of how much you might be able to borrow, while pre-approval involves a more thorough review of your financial history. A pre-approval gives you a better idea of your actual budget and shows sellers that you're serious.

Documents Needed for Pre-Approval

To get pre-approved, you'll need to provide:

Proof of income (W-2s, tax returns)

Bank statements

Credit report

Employment verification

How Pre-Approval Affects Your Home Search

Once you're pre-approved, you'll have a better idea of how much you can afford. This allows you to focus your search on homes within your budget, making the process more efficient.

Chapter 5: Choosing the Right Real Estate Agent

A knowledgeable real estate agent can be your greatest asset during the homebuying process.

Why You Need a Real Estate Agent

An experienced agent will help you navigate the market, negotiate offers, and handle paperwork. They'll also have access to listings you might not find on your own.

How to Find a Good Agent

Look for an agent with experience in your desired area. Ask for recommendations from friends or family, and read online reviews. Schedule interviews with potential agents to see if they're a good fit.

What to Expect from Your Agent

Your agent should help you find homes, set up viewings, and guide you through making offers. They'll also handle negotiations with sellers and other agents.

(Continue developing the rest of the ebook in the same format for each chapter, expanding on topics like house hunting, inspections, closing, and post-purchase responsibilities.)

Chapter 6: The House Hunt Begins

House Hunting Tips: What to Look For & Bidding Strategies

When you're house hunting, it's important to have a clear plan. From knowing what to look for in a home to crafting a smart bidding strategy, here are key tips to guide you through the process.

House Hunting Tips

1. Set Your Budget

Pre-Approval: Get pre-approved for a mortgage before starting your search. This gives you a clear understanding of your budget and signals to sellers that you're a serious buyer.

Hidden Costs: Factor in other costs like property taxes, insurance, utilities, and potential HOA fees when determining what you can afford.

2. Define Your Needs vs. Wants

Non-Negotiables: List the features that are must-haves, like the number of bedrooms or proximity to work or school.

Nice-to-Haves: These are features you'd like but could live without—such as a large yard or modern finishes. Prioritize your list to help you make decisions quickly.

3. Do Your Research

Neighborhood Insight: Visit neighborhoods at different times of the day to get a true feel for the area. Check for things like traffic, noise, and general vibe.

Market Trends: Stay updated on the real estate trends in your desired area. Is it a buyer's market or a seller's market? This can influence your bidding strategy.

4. Attend Open Houses & Showings

Visualize Potential: Sometimes a home might not seem perfect at first glance but has potential with minor changes. Try to visualize how you can personalize the space.

Check for Signs of Problems: Look for issues like water damage, cracks in the foundation, uneven floors, or outdated systems (like plumbing or electrical). A home inspection will catch these, but it's good to have an eye out during showings.

5. Think Long Term

Future Growth: Consider your long-term goals. Is this a home you plan to stay in for years, or are you looking for something temporary? Understanding this helps refine your search and investment choices.

Resale Value: Look for properties that have good resale potential, especially if you plan to sell in a few years. Location, layout, and amenities play a big role in future value.

What to Look for in a House

1. Condition of Major Systems

Roof, HVAC, Electrical, Plumbing: These are costly to replace, so look for signs of aging or problems. Ask when these systems were last updated or replaced.

Foundation: Look for cracks, uneven floors, or doors and windows that don't close properly, which could indicate foundation problems.

2. Floor Plan & Layout

Flow of Space: Does the layout make sense for your lifestyle? An open floor plan may be ideal for some, while others prefer more compartmentalized rooms for privacy.

Room Sizes: Pay attention to the size of the rooms, not just the number. Small bedrooms or a cramped kitchen could be a deal breaker.

3. Natural Light

Windows & Orientation: Homes with plenty of windows and good exposure to natural light tend to feel more welcoming and can save on energy costs.

4. Storage Space

Closets, Attic, Garage: Check for adequate storage. Homes without enough storage space can feel cramped over time, especially for growing families.

5. Potential for Upgrades

Cosmetic Changes: Look for homes that need only cosmetic upgrades like paint or flooring. These are usually more affordable than homes that need structural repairs.

Room to Expand: If you plan to stay for many years, consider whether the home has space to grow—such as an unfinished basement, attic, or room for an extension.

Bidding Strategies

1. Know the Market

Buyer's vs. Seller's Market: In a buyer's market, you have more negotiating power. In a seller's market, homes may receive multiple offers, so you'll need to be more competitive.

Days on Market: If a home has been sitting for a while, the seller might be more open to negotiation. A newly listed home might require a more aggressive bid.

2. Make a Competitive Offer

Be Realistic: Offering too low in a competitive market could cost you the house. Use recent comparable sales ("comps") to guide your offer.

Escalation Clause: In highly competitive situations, consider adding an escalation clause that automatically increases your bid up to a maximum limit if other offers come in higher.

3. Personalize Your Offer

Letter to the Seller: A personal letter to the seller explaining why you love the house can sometimes help your offer stand out, especially if the seller is emotionally attached to the home.

Flexible Closing Date: Offering a flexible closing date can also make your bid more appealing. Sellers may have specific timing needs, and accommodating them could give you an edge.

4. Include an Inspection Contingency

Protect Yourself: An inspection contingency allows you to back out or renegotiate if significant problems are uncovered during the home inspection. While you want to be competitive, this is a key protection for buyers.

5. Be Prepared to Act Fast

Pre-Approval & Funds Ready: Make sure you have your mortgage pre-approval and down payment funds ready to go. Being prepared to move quickly can make a difference, especially in fast-moving markets.

No Contingencies (Carefully): In very competitive situations, some buyers choose to waive certain contingencies (like a mortgage or appraisal contingency) to make their offer stronger. However, this carries risk and should be carefully considered with your real estate agent.

By being prepared, knowing what to look for, and crafting a solid bidding strategy, you'll have a better chance of securing the home that's right for you, at a price that makes sense.

Chapter 7: Making An Offer On A Home

Understanding the Home Offer Process

The home offer process can be both exciting and nerve-wracking. Here's a breakdown of the steps involved:

1. Preparing Your Offer

Determine Your Offer Price: Your real estate agent will help you decide on a competitive offer price based on recent comparable sales ("comps") in the area, the condition of the home, and the current market conditions (e.g., buyer's or seller's market).

Earnest Money Deposit: This is a deposit you make to show the seller that you are serious about buying the home. It is typically 1-3% of the purchase price and is held in escrow until closing. If the sale falls through for valid reasons, you may get this deposit back.

Contract Terms: Your offer will include details such as the purchase price, the amount of earnest money, the closing date, and any contingencies (e.g., inspection, financing, or appraisal).

2: Submitting the Offer

Writing the Offer: Your real estate agent will help you draft a formal written offer. This includes the offer price, any contingencies, and the terms of the purchase.

Presentation to Seller: The seller will review the offer, often with their agent. Depending on the market, the seller may receive multiple offers at once.

3. Negotiation

Counteroffers: The seller can accept your offer as is, reject it outright, or counteroffer. In a counteroffer, they may request a higher price, different terms, or adjustments to contingencies.

Negotiation Period: You and the seller may go back and forth until both parties agree on the terms. Your real estate agent will help you strategize during this time.

4. Acceptance

Accepted Offer: Once both parties agree on the price and terms, the seller signs the offer, making it a legally binding contract. The home then goes into escrow, which is a neutral third-party account that holds funds and documents until closing.

Opening Escrow: Earnest money is typically deposited into the escrow account at this time. The process of inspections, appraisals, and securing financing begins.

Common Mistakes to Avoid in the Home Offer Process

1. Lowball Offers in a Seller's Market

The Mistake: Offering a price significantly lower than the asking price in a competitive market.

Why It's a Problem: In a hot market, lowball offers are unlikely to be accepted. You could lose out on your dream home, and the seller may not even counter your offer if they find it insulting.

2. Skipping Pre-Approval

The Mistake: Making an offer without being pre-approved for a mortgage.

Why It's a Problem: Sellers are less likely to take your offer seriously if you don't have proof of your ability to finance the purchase. Pre-approval gives you a clear budget and strengthens your position as a buyer.

3. Ignoring the "Comps"

The Mistake: Not considering recent comparable sales when determining your offer price.

Why It's a Problem: Basing your offer on emotions rather than market data can lead to overpaying or losing the bid. Researching comps ensures you make a competitive but reasonable offer.

4. Being Unprepared for Multiple Offers

The Mistake: Assuming there will be no competition for the home.

Why It's a Problem: You might miss out on a home because you weren't prepared to increase your offer or didn't include an escalation clause. Always ask your agent about the likelihood of multiple offers and plan accordingly.

5. Overlooking Contingencies

The Mistake: Waiving contingencies to make your offer more attractive without understanding the risks.

Why It's a Problem: Waiving key contingencies like the inspection or financing contingency can put you at financial risk if something goes wrong (e.g., finding major defects or failing to secure financing).

The Role of Contingencies

Contingencies are clauses in the offer that allow you to back out of the deal under certain conditions without losing your earnest money deposit. They provide essential protection for buyers. Here are the most common contingencies:

1. Financing Contingency

What It Is: This clause allows you to cancel the contract if you are unable to secure financing (a mortgage) within a specified period.

Why It's Important: If you lose financing for any reason—such as an issue with your credit or the bank—this contingency allows you to exit the deal without penalty.

2. Inspection Contingency

What It Is: This allows the buyer to have the home professionally inspected and request repairs or renegotiate the price based on the findings. You can walk away from the deal if the home has significant issues.

Why It's Important: The inspection contingency protects you from buying a home with costly, undiscovered problems like faulty plumbing, a damaged roof, or structural issues.

3. Appraisal Contingency

What It Is: This allows you to back out of the deal if the home appraises for less than the purchase price.

Why It's Important: If the appraisal comes in lower than your offer, your lender may not cover the full amount of the mortgage.

You may have to renegotiate the price or pay the difference out of pocket.

4. Home Sale Contingency

What It Is: This contingency allows you to back out of the deal if you are unable to sell your current home before closing on the new one.

Why It's Important: If you need the proceeds from selling your existing home to purchase the new one, this contingency protects you from owning two homes at once or facing financial strain.

5. Title Contingency

What It Is: This allows you to back out if there are issues with the title of the property (e.g., unresolved liens, disputes over ownership).

Why It's Important: Ensuring that the property has clear and marketable title is crucial to avoid legal issues or ownership disputes in the future.

Understanding the home offer process, avoiding common mistakes, and carefully considering contingencies will help protect you from potential risks. A well-thought-out offer backed by solid contingencies ensures that you are in a strong position, both in securing your dream home and in safeguarding your investment. Having a knowledgeable real estate agent by your side will also guide you through negotiations and help you make informed decisions.

Chapter 8: The Home Inspection

A home inspection is one of the most important steps in the home-buying process. It provides a detailed assessment of the property's condition and can reveal hidden issues that may affect the value and safety of the home. Understanding why it's crucial, how to hire a qualified inspector, and how to negotiate based on the inspection results will help you make informed decisions and protect your investment.

Why the Home Inspection Is Crucial

1. Uncover Hidden Issues

Major Defects: The inspection can reveal significant issues that may not be visible during a standard showing, such as structural problems, faulty electrical wiring, plumbing issues, or roof damage. These defects can be costly to fix and may impact your decision to proceed with the purchase.

Safety Concerns: Inspectors check for safety hazards like mold, asbestos, radon, lead paint, or improper electrical work that could pose risks to your health and safety.

2. Leverage for Negotiation

Repairs or Price Reduction: The findings from the inspection give you leverage to negotiate repairs or ask for a price reduction. If serious problems are found, you may request that the seller fix them before closing or provide a credit toward the cost of repairs.

Walk Away Option: If the inspection reveals issues that are too costly or complex to address, you can back out of the deal (if you have an inspection contingency) without losing your earnest money.

3. Peace of Mind

Confidence in Your Purchase: A thorough inspection helps you understand the true condition of the home and what maintenance or repairs will be needed. This can give you peace of mind that you're making a sound investment.

How to Hire a Good Home Inspector

Choosing the right home inspector is crucial to ensuring a thorough and accurate assessment of the property. Here's how to find a qualified inspector:

1. Look for Qualifications

Licensing and Certification: Check if the inspector is licensed and certified by reputable organizations, such as the American Society of Home Inspectors (ASHI), the International Association of Certified Home Inspectors (InterNACHI), or the National Institute of Building Inspectors (NIBI). These certifications indicate that the inspector has undergone proper training and adheres to industry standards.

Experience: Ask how long they have been inspecting homes and how many inspections they've completed. An experienced inspector will be more likely to spot issues that could be overlooked by someone with less experience.

2. Ask for References

Client Reviews: Request references from past clients and check online reviews on sites like Google, Yelp, or Angie's List. Positive feedback from previous clients can give you confidence in the inspector's work.

Ask Realtors for Recommendations: A trusted real estate agent can often recommend inspectors they've worked with in the past, but be cautious—make sure the inspector is truly independent and will prioritize your interests over the sale.

3. Review a Sample Report

Thoroughness of Report: Ask potential inspectors for a sample inspection report. A good report should be detailed, clearly written, and include photos and explanations of any issues found. It should cover all major systems of the home, including roofing, plumbing, electrical, HVAC, foundation, and more.

Turnaround Time: Find out how long it takes the inspector to deliver the final report. You'll want someone who can provide a comprehensive report within a day or two, allowing you to move forward with negotiations or other decisions promptly.

4. Discuss What's Included

Scope of Inspection: Confirm what the inspection will cover, such as the roof, foundation, insulation, electrical systems, and plumbing. Some inspectors may offer additional services for an extra fee, like radon testing, mold testing, or termite inspections.

Attendance: It's often a good idea to attend the inspection if possible. This allows you to ask questions on-site and get a better understanding of any potential problems.

Negotiating Repairs and Closing Costs After the Inspection

Once the inspection is complete, the next step is negotiating with the seller based on the inspection report. Here's how to navigate this process:

1. Prioritize Repairs

Major Issues First: Focus on negotiating repairs for major issues such as structural defects, roof problems, plumbing leaks, or safety hazards. These are often the most expensive and critical to address.

Cosmetic Issues: Cosmetic issues like paint touch-ups or small drywall repairs are usually not worth negotiating, especially in a competitive market. Prioritize the most significant problems that could impact the home's value or safety.

2. Options for Negotiating

Ask for Seller-Paid Repairs: You can request that the seller make specific repairs before closing. This is common for larger issues like a damaged roof or broken HVAC system. Make sure that repairs are completed by licensed professionals and that you receive documentation confirming the work.

Request a Price Reduction or Credit: Instead of asking the seller to make the repairs, you can negotiate a price reduction or ask for a credit toward closing costs. This allows you to control the repair process after closing and ensures the work is done to your standards.

Home Warranty: You might negotiate for the seller to purchase a home warranty, which can cover the cost of repairing or replacing systems and appliances for the first year of ownership.

3. Be Realistic

Market Conditions: In a seller's market, sellers may be less willing to make repairs or offer concessions, especially if there are multiple offers. In these situations, focus on the most critical repairs or consider if the home is still worth purchasing without the seller's help.

Negotiation Approach: Be respectful and reasonable in your requests. A hardline stance on minor issues could result in losing the deal. Work with your real estate agent to determine the best approach for the current market and the specifics of the property.

4. Reinspections

Verify Repairs: If the seller agrees to make repairs, consider requesting a reinspection by your home inspector before closing to verify that the work was completed properly. This ensures that there are no lingering issues when you take ownership.

Closing Costs and Negotiations

In addition to repairs, the inspection process can also open the door for negotiating closing costs:

1. Ask for Closing Cost Credits

Inspection Credit: If the inspection uncovers significant issues, you can request that the seller contribute toward your closing costs rather than making repairs. This credit can help cover expenses like title insurance, lender fees, and prepaid property taxes.

2. Leverage Inspection Findings

Bargaining Power: Major inspection findings can give you leverage in asking the seller to cover more of your closing costs. This is especially useful if the seller is unable or unwilling to address certain repairs.

3. Understand Closing Costs

Be Prepared: Make sure you know the typical closing costs in your area and budget accordingly. Closing costs usually range from 2% to 5% of the home's purchase price and include fees such as loan origination, title insurance, appraisals, and escrow fees

A home inspection is a critical step in ensuring you are making a sound investment. By hiring a qualified inspector, prioritizing necessary repairs, and negotiating thoughtfully, you can protect yourself from future headaches and financial burdens. The inspection not only provides valuable insights into the home's condition but also empowers you to negotiate repairs, price adjustments, and potentially even closing cost credits.

Chapter 9: Securing Your Mortgage

Securing a mortgage is a key step in the home-buying process. It involves several important decisions, including locking in your interest rate, choosing your mortgage terms, and undergoing the underwriting process. Here's a breakdown of what to expect at each stage:

Securing Your Mortgage

Once you've found the home you want to buy, it's time to secure financing through a mortgage. This process can take several steps, but it all begins with selecting the right loan product and lender.

Get Pre-Approved

Pre-Approval: Before you make an offer on a home, it's a good idea to get pre-approved for a mortgage. This involves submitting basic financial information—such as income, credit history, and debt levels—to a lender who will give you an estimate of how much you can borrow.

Benefit: Pre-approval shows sellers you are serious and financially capable of buying the home, giving you an edge in competitive markets.

Choosing the Right Mortgage

Fixed-Rate vs. Adjustable-Rate Mortgages: The two main types of mortgages are fixed-rate and adjustable-rate (ARM). A fixed-rate mortgage locks in your interest rate for the life of the loan, offering stability in payments. An adjustable-rate mortgage may have a lower initial rate but can fluctuate over time, depending on market conditions.

Loan Term (15, 20, 30 Years): Mortgage terms vary in length. Shorter terms, like 15 or 20 years, typically have higher monthly payments but lower overall interest costs. Longer terms, like 30 years, offer lower monthly payments but higher total interest.

Down Payment: Consider how much you can afford for a down payment. The traditional 20% down payment allows you to avoid private mortgage insurance (PMI), but there are loan options available with lower down payment requirements.

Locking in Your Interest Rate

Once your mortgage application is in process, locking in your interest rate is a critical step. Interest rates fluctuate daily, so timing can affect your mortgage payments significantly over the life of the loan.

What is an Interest Rate Lock?

Rate Lock Defined: An interest rate lock is a guarantee from the lender that your mortgage will have a specific interest rate, regardless of market fluctuations, as long as the loan closes within a specified period (usually 30-60 days).

When to Lock: You typically lock in your rate after your mortgage application is accepted but before the loan is finalized. Locking in early protects you from potential rate increases.

How Long Should You Lock In?

Standard Lock Periods: Most rate locks are between 30 and 60 days. You want to ensure that your rate lock period covers the time it will take to close the loan.

Extended Rate Lock: If your closing is expected to take longer (such as in the case of new construction), some lenders offer extended rate locks for up to 120 days or more. However, extended locks may come with additional fees.

Floating Your Rate

Floating: Instead of locking in your rate right away, some buyers choose to "float" the rate with the hope that rates will decrease before closing. This can be risky, as rates could also increase, potentially raising your monthly payment.

Finalizing Your Mortgage Terms

Finalizing your mortgage involves choosing the specific details of your loan, including the loan type, term length, and any additional features. Here's what to consider:

Loan Type

Conventional Loan: These are not insured or guaranteed by the federal government. They typically require higher credit scores and larger down payments but may offer more flexibility.

FHA Loan: Backed by the Federal Housing Administration, FHA loans are more accessible to first-time buyers or those with lower credit scores, with down payments as low as 3.5%.

VA Loan: Available to veterans and active-duty service members, VA loans often offer favorable terms, such as no down payment and no PMI.

USDA Loan: These loans are aimed at rural buyers and offer zero down payment options, but are limited to specific geographic areas.

Term Length

Short-Term vs. Long-Term: Shorter terms (e.g., 15 years) usually have lower interest rates but require higher monthly payments. Longer terms (e.g., 30 years) reduce monthly payments but increase the total interest paid over the life of the loan.

Points and Fees

Discount Points: Buyers can choose to pay discount points to lower their interest rate. One point typically costs 1% of the loan amount and can reduce the interest rate by a small percentage.

Closing Costs: Finalizing your loan will involve closing costs, which typically range from 2% to 5% of the loan amount. These costs include lender fees, appraisal fees, title insurance, and more.

What to Expect During Underwriting

The underwriting process is where your lender verifies all of your financial information and assesses the risk of lending you money. It's one of the final steps before your loan is approved.

Steps in Underwriting

1. Verification of Information

Income and Employment: The underwriter will verify your income and employment by reviewing your pay stubs, W-2 forms, and tax returns. They may also contact your employer directly to confirm your employment status.

Credit Check: A thorough review of your credit history and credit score is conducted to assess your ability to manage debt and determine the terms of your loan.

Debt-to-Income Ratio (DTI): Your lender will calculate your DTI ratio to ensure that your monthly debts (including the new mortgage) do not exceed a certain percentage of your monthly income.

2. Appraisal

Home Appraisal: An appraisal will be ordered to assess the value of the home you're purchasing. The underwriter uses this appraisal to ensure that the loan amount does not exceed the value of the property, which protects the lender.

3. Title Search

Clear Title: A title search is conducted to ensure there are no legal issues (e.g., unpaid taxes, liens) that could impact your ownership of the property. The lender will require you to have title insurance to protect against any title defects.

4. Review of Funds

Down Payment and Reserves: The underwriter will verify that you have the necessary funds for the down payment, closing costs, and any required cash reserves. They may ask for recent bank statements and documentation of where the funds came from.

Possible Outcomes of Underwriting

Conditional Approval: Most loans receive conditional approval, meaning that the underwriter approves the loan, but certain conditions must be met (such as providing additional documentation or resolving outstanding issues with the property).

Final Approval (Clear to Close): Once all conditions are met, the loan is "clear to close," and you can proceed to closing.

Denial: If the underwriter finds issues that cannot be resolved, the loan may be denied. In this case, you'll want to discuss with your lender what can be done to remedy the situation.

Securing your mortgage involves a series of decisions and steps that must be carefully managed. Locking in your interest rate ensures stability in your payments, and finalizing the terms of your loan tailors your mortgage to your financial needs. The underwriting process is the final verification step before your loan is approved. By understanding each stage and working closely with your lender, you can navigate the mortgage process smoothly and ensure that you are financially prepared for homeownership.

Chapter 10: Closing The Deal

Closing on a home is the final step in the buying process, where ownership officially transfers from the seller to the buyer. Understanding the costs involved, reviewing your closing disclosures, and preparing for the final walkthrough and closing day will help you avoid surprises and ensure the process goes smoothly. Here's what you need to know.

Understanding Closing Costs

Closing costs are the fees and expenses you must pay when finalizing the purchase of a home. These costs typically range from 2% to 5% of the home's purchase price and can vary depending on your location and the specifics of your loan. Here are the most common closing costs:

1. Loan-Related Costs

Origination Fee: This fee covers the lender's cost of processing your loan. It's typically around 0.5% to 1% of the loan amount.

Discount Points: Optional fees paid to reduce your interest rate. One point costs 1% of the loan amount and lowers your interest rate by a small amount.

Appraisal Fee: The cost for a professional appraisal to determine the value of the home (usually $300-$500).

2. Prepaid Costs

Property Taxes: You may need to prepay property taxes at closing, depending on when they are due. This is usually a few months' worth of taxes.

Homeowners Insurance: Lenders often require that you prepay the first year of homeowners insurance at closing.

Mortgage Insurance (PMI or MIP): If you're putting down less than 20%, you'll likely need to pay mortgage insurance premiums upfront (either Private Mortgage Insurance or FHA's Mortgage Insurance Premium).

3. Title and Legal Fees

Title Search and Title Insurance: A title search ensures there are no legal claims against the property. Title insurance protects both you and the lender against future claims. Costs vary but can be a significant portion of your closing costs.

Attorney Fees: In some states, an attorney must oversee the closing. Their fees can vary widely depending on the complexity of the transaction.

4. Recording and Transfer Fees

Recording Fees: These are paid to the local government for recording the change in property ownership.

Transfer Taxes: Some states and municipalities charge a transfer tax based on the purchase price of the home.

5. Other Fees

Escrow Fees: Fees for the escrow service that holds funds and documents until the sale is complete.

Survey Fee: Some lenders require a survey to confirm property boundaries.

Reviewing Your Closing Disclosures

Three days before closing, your lender is required to provide you with the Closing Disclosure (CD). This document outlines the final details of your loan, including the loan amount, interest rate, monthly payments, and the exact closing costs.

Key Sections to Review

Loan Terms: Double-check the loan amount, interest rate, loan term, and whether your loan has a prepayment penalty or balloon payment.

Projected Payments: Review your total monthly payment, which includes your principal, interest, taxes, and insurance. Ensure this aligns with your expectations.

Closing Costs: Compare the closing costs listed on the CD with the Loan Estimate you received when you first applied for the mortgage. If any costs have increased significantly, ask your lender for an explanation.

Cash to Close: This is the total amount you will need to bring to closing. Make sure you have these funds ready to transfer, often through a certified check or wire transfer.

Take your time reviewing the Closing Disclosure. If anything is unclear, ask your lender or attorney for clarification before the closing day.

Preparing for the Final Walkthrough

The final walkthrough usually takes place the day before or the morning of closing. It's your last chance to inspect the home before taking ownership.

Purpose of the Final Walkthrough

Confirm Repairs: If the seller agreed to make repairs after the inspection, check that the work has been completed to your satisfaction. Ask for receipts for the repairs if necessary.

Ensure the Condition of the Home: Make sure the property is in the same condition as when you agreed to buy it. Look for any new damage or missing fixtures/appliances.

Check Systems and Appliances: Turn on faucets, lights, and appliances to ensure everything is functioning properly. Also, test the HVAC system and check for any signs of water damage.

Verify Removal of Seller's Items: Ensure the seller has removed all personal belongings (unless something was specifically included in the sale) and that the home is clean and ready for move-in.

If you find any significant issues during the walkthrough, notify your real estate agent immediately. They will help you negotiate a solution with the seller, which could involve a delay in closing or a credit for the cost of repairs.

What to Expect on Closing Day

Closing day is when you sign all the necessary paperwork and officially become the owner of the home. The closing typically takes place at a title company office, escrow office, or attorney's office, depending on your location. Here's what to expect:

1. Who Will Be There

Buyer and Seller: In many cases, the buyer and seller do not meet in person at closing. If both parties are present, it's usually a brief and cordial interaction.

Closing Agent or Escrow Officer: This person oversees the closing process, ensures all documents are signed, and manages the transfer of funds.

Your Real Estate Agent: Your agent will likely attend closing to support you and answer any questions.

Attorney: If your state requires an attorney at closing, or if you hired one, they will be present to review documents and represent your interests.

Lender's Representative: Sometimes, a representative from your lender will attend, but this isn't always necessary.

2. What You Need to Bring

Identification: Bring a government-issued ID, such as a driver's license or passport, as it will be required to sign legal documents.

Cash to Close: You'll need to provide the funds for your down payment and closing costs. This is usually done via a wire transfer or certified check. Your lender or title company will provide you with instructions for making this payment.

Closing Disclosure: Bring your copy of the Closing Disclosure to compare with the final documents you'll be signing.

3. Documents You'll Sign

Promissory Note: This is your agreement to repay the loan under the specified terms.

Mortgage/Deed of Trust: This document secures the loan and grants the lender a lien on the property.

Deed: The deed transfers ownership from the seller to you. After signing, it will be recorded with the local government.

Closing Disclosure: You'll sign a final version of the Closing Disclosure, confirming the terms of the loan and the costs involved.

Other Documents: Depending on your state and lender, there may be additional forms, such as affidavits, tax forms, and title insurance documents.

4. Final Steps

Review the Documents: Take your time reviewing all documents before signing. If anything is unclear or incorrect, don't hesitate to ask questions or request corrections.

Transfer of Keys: Once all documents are signed and funds are transferred, the seller will hand over the keys to the property.

Title and Deed Recording: After closing, the title company or attorney will file the deed with the county, making you the official owner of the home.

Closing on a home is an exciting but detailed process that requires careful preparation. Understanding your closing costs, thoroughly reviewing your closing disclosures, and completing a final walkthrough will help ensure a smooth and successful transaction. On closing day, be prepared to sign a variety of documents and verify that all terms match what was agreed upon. By knowing what to expect, you can avoid surprises and feel confident as you take ownership of your new home.

Chapter 11: After You Buy

Congratulations on buying your home! Once the closing process is complete and you have the keys in hand, there are several steps to take to ensure a smooth transition into your new property. This guide will help you move in, set up utilities and services, and take care of essential home maintenance as a new homeowner.

Moving In: Step-by-Step

Moving into a new home can be both exciting and overwhelming. Here's a step-by-step approach to make the process smoother:

Step 1: Change the Locks

Why: For security reasons, it's a good idea to change the locks on all doors to ensure you have the only keys to your home.

What to Do: Hire a locksmith or, if you're comfortable, purchase new locksets from a hardware store and replace them yourself.

Step 2: Clean Your New Home

Why: Even if the home was cleaned before closing, a thorough deep clean can give you peace of mind and a fresh start.

What to Do: Focus on high-touch areas like light switches, door handles, and bathrooms. Consider hiring a professional cleaning service for carpets and floors.

Step 3: Make a Moving Checklist

Why: Staying organized will help ensure that nothing is forgotten during your move.

What to Do: Create a checklist that includes packing, scheduling movers (or renting a truck if you're doing it yourself), and transferring important items like valuables and documents separately.

Step 4: Plan Your Unpacking

Why: Unpacking strategically helps prevent chaos.

What to Do: Unpack essentials first (kitchen, bathrooms, and bedding). Label boxes by room to make unpacking easier. If possible, set up one room (like the bedroom) as a sanctuary to escape to when the rest of the house is in disarray.

Setting Up Utilities and Services

One of the most important steps in moving into a new home is ensuring that all your utilities and essential services are up and running.

Utilities to Set Up

Electricity and Gas: Contact the utility providers in your area to set up service or transfer it into your name. Ask about meter readings and billing cycles.

Water and Sewer: This is usually handled by the city or municipality. Make sure to contact the appropriate office to establish your account and set up billing.

Internet and Cable: Shop around for the best internet and cable service providers in your area. Be sure to schedule installation appointments ahead of time, as there can sometimes be a wait.

Garbage and Recycling: Determine which day of the week garbage and recycling are collected. You may need to set up service with a waste management company if it's not provided by the city.

Home Services to Consider

Home Security: Consider installing a home security system for added peace of mind. Many companies offer DIY systems or professional installation, depending on your needs.

Lawn Care and Landscaping: If your new home has a yard, decide whether you'll maintain it yourself or hire a landscaping company. In colder climates, you may also need to arrange for snow removal in the winter.

Pest Control: It's a good idea to have a pest control service inspect your home, especially if the property was vacant for a while before you moved in.

Home Maintenance Tips for New Homeowners

Owning a home comes with responsibilities, especially when it comes to regular maintenance. Keeping up with small tasks can help you avoid expensive repairs down the road. Here are some essential home maintenance tips for new homeowners:

Monthly Maintenance Tasks

Inspect HVAC Filters: Check and replace HVAC filters regularly to keep your heating and cooling systems running efficiently. Dirty filters can increase energy costs and reduce air quality.

Clean Kitchen Vent Hood: Clean the vent hood over your stove to ensure it's free of grease buildup, which can be a fire hazard.

Check for Leaks: Regularly inspect under sinks, around toilets, and in basements or crawlspaces for signs of leaks. Early detection can prevent water damage.

Seasonal Maintenance Tasks

Spring:

Inspect the Roof: Check for missing shingles, leaks, or damage that may have occurred over the winter.

Gutter Cleaning: Clear out leaves and debris from your gutters to ensure proper drainage.

Exterior Maintenance: Inspect and repaint or repair any worn or damaged areas on the exterior of your home, including trim, siding, and windows.

Summer:

Lawn Care and Landscaping: Keep your lawn mowed and gardens watered. Consider adding mulch to retain moisture and keep weeds at bay.

Check Air Conditioning: Ensure your AC is functioning properly before the heat of summer sets in. Schedule professional maintenance if necessary.

Fall:

Furnace Maintenance: Before cold weather arrives, have your furnace serviced to ensure it's ready for winter. Replace the filter and check for any issues.

Winterize Outdoor Faucets: Disconnect garden hoses, drain outdoor faucets, and install faucet covers to prevent freezing.

Chimney Cleaning: If you have a fireplace, have the chimney cleaned to remove any creosote buildup and reduce the risk of chimney fires.

Winter:

Inspect and Seal Drafts: Check for drafts around windows and doors. Install weather stripping or caulking to improve energy efficiency and keep heating costs down.

Test Smoke and Carbon Monoxide Detectors: Regularly test all detectors in your home and replace batteries as needed. This should be done at least twice a year.

Annual Maintenance Tasks

Deep Clean Appliances: Once a year, deep clean your refrigerator coils, dishwasher, and washing machine to ensure they continue running efficiently.

Check Water Heater: Flush your water heater to remove sediment buildup, which can affect its efficiency and lifespan. If your water heater is older, consider replacing it to avoid unexpected breakdowns.

Inspect Foundation and Crawl Spaces: Check for cracks in your foundation, as well as any signs of moisture in crawl spaces or basements, which can lead to structural issues over time.

Service Your Septic System: If you have a septic system, have it inspected and pumped every 3-5 years to prevent issues like backups or leaks.

Personalizing Your New Home

Once the essentials are taken care of, it's time to make your new house feel like home.

Paint and Decor

Why: A fresh coat of paint can instantly change the feel of a room and reflect your style.

What to Do: Choose colors that match your aesthetic and paint the rooms before you fully unpack to avoid shifting furniture multiple times.

Organize Your Spaces

Why: Organizing your home from the start makes it easier to maintain cleanliness and functionality.

What to Do: Invest in storage solutions, label boxes, and create systems for organization in closets, kitchens, and garages.

Get to Know Your Neighborhood

Why: Knowing your neighbors and the local community can help you feel more at home and connected.

What to Do: Take walks around your neighborhood, introduce yourself to neighbors, and explore local shops, parks, and restaurants.

Moving into a new home is a significant milestone that comes with a mix of excitement and responsibility. Following these steps for moving in, setting up utilities and services, and staying on top of maintenance will help ensure that you settle in smoothly and enjoy your new space. By keeping up with routine maintenance tasks, you can protect your investment and avoid costly repairs in the future.

Conclusion

Becoming a first-time homebuyer is an exciting milestone that marks the beginning of a new chapter in your life. While the process can be overwhelming, the rewards of homeownership are substantial, providing not only a place to call your own but also a potential investment for the future.

As you navigate the journey from searching for your ideal home to closing the deal, it's essential to stay informed and organized. Understanding the various stages of homebuying—such as financing, making offers, and closing—will empower you to make confident decisions. Additionally, recognizing the importance of proper inspections, securing a favorable mortgage, and planning for ongoing maintenance will help you protect your investment and ensure a comfortable living environment.

Embrace the learning curve that comes with being a new homeowner. Each step presents opportunities to build equity, create lasting memories, and personalize your space to fit your lifestyle. Remember that it's okay to seek guidance from professionals, whether they are real estate agents, mortgage brokers, or home inspectors. Surrounding yourself with knowledgeable support can help mitigate risks and ease concerns.

Ultimately, the journey of homeownership is about finding a space that reflects who you are and where you envision your life unfolding. With careful planning, research, and a positive mindset, you can turn your dream of owning a home into a reality, paving the way for a bright future in your new abode. Welcome to the rewarding world of homeownership!

www.ingramcontent.com/pod-product-compliance
Lightning Source LLC
Chambersburg PA
CBHW030051230526
45471CB00003B/1036